Farm
Follow-the-Dots

Barbara Soloff Levy

DOVER PUBLICATIONS, INC.
Mineola, New York

Bibliographical Note

Little Farm Follow-the-Dots is a new work, first published by Dover
Publications, Inc., in 2005.

International Standard Book Number
ISBN-13: 978-0-486-44050-7
ISBN-10: 0-486-44050-8

Manufactured in the United States by Courier Corporation
44050805
www.doverpublications.com

NOTE

This little book has lots of pictures of animals, people, and things that you might see on a farm. To see the pictures, though, you will need to connect the dots! First, read the hint below the puzzle and try to figure out what you will see when the picture is complete. Then, using a pencil, start at dot number 1 and draw a line to dot number 2, and from dot number 2 to dot number 3, and so on, in number order. When you have followed all of the dots, you will see your picture. At the back of the book is a list of what you will find in the puzzles, just in case you need some help. Are you ready to have some puzzle fun? Get your pencil out and let's get started!

He lives on the farm and works there every day with his wife, son, and daughter. Who is he? Follow the dots to find out!

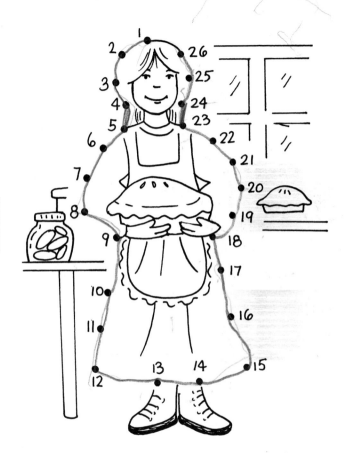

She works every day with her husband to run the farm.
Connect the dots to see her picture.

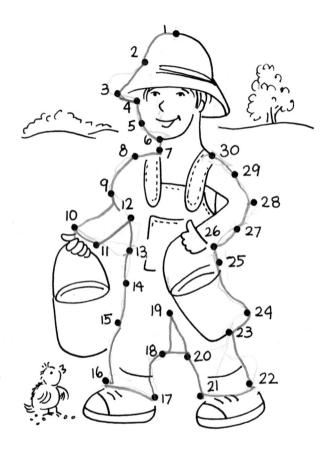

He lives with his parents on the farm and helps out
with many of the chores.

She feeds the animals and has her daily chores as well.

This farm animal is pink and plump and has a curly tail.
The noise it makes sounds like "Oink, Oink!"

These farm animal babies like to take a mud bath.
Follow the dots to find out who they are.

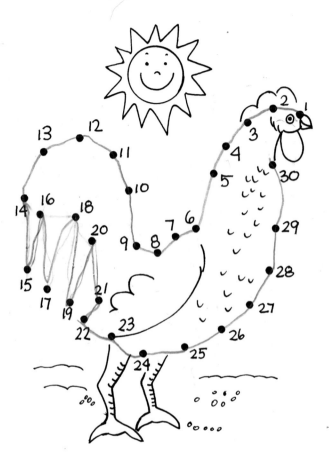

Each morning, this bird wakes up the farm
with its cry of "Cock-a-doodle-do!"

This mother bird pecks at grain in the barnyard
when it is time to eat.

Small and fluffy, this yellow bird follows its
mother to find food.

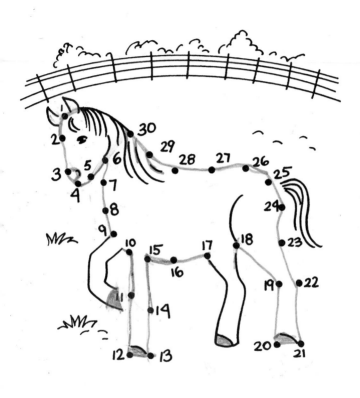

You can find this animal galloping through the field.
Follow the dots to see what it is.

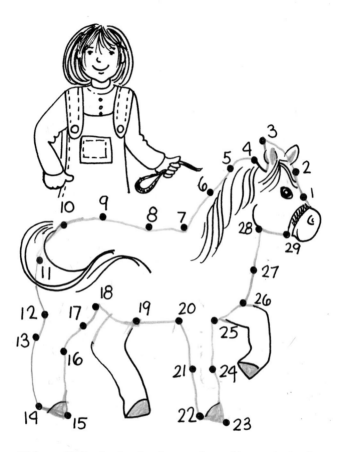

This medium-sized animal can take a rider on its back.
It has a strong body and a long tail.

14

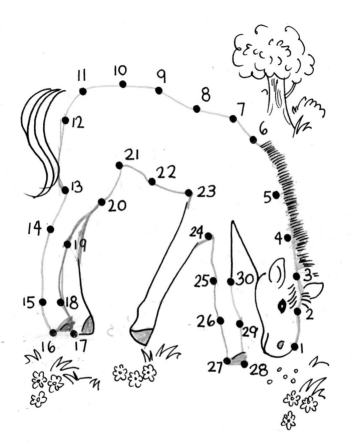

When it grows up, this animal will trot and gallop
just like its parents.

This baby farm animal says, "Baa, Baa."
It has hoofs and a soft, curly coat.

The farmer cuts off this animal's thick coat, and his wife
spins it into yarn. What animal is it?

You will find this animal munching on whatever
it can find. It's not picky!

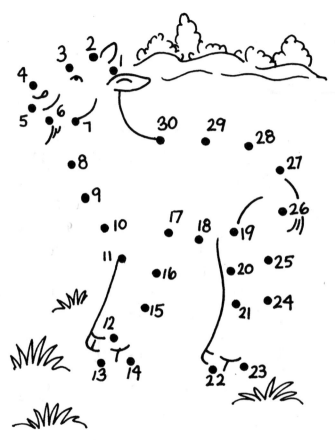

This farm animal baby has whiskers on its chin
and will be growing horns soon.

This animal loves to chase mice.
Connect the dots to see its picture.

These farm animal babies purr when they're happy.
They have soft fur and long tails.

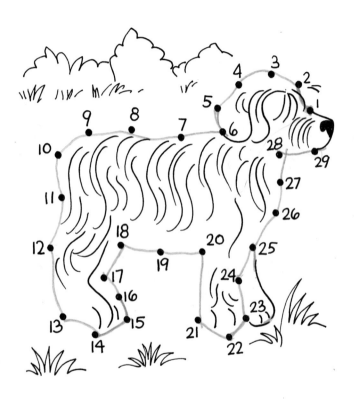

This animal helps the farmer herd the sheep.
You might hear it barking.

Another farm creature helps the farmer
round up some of his animals.

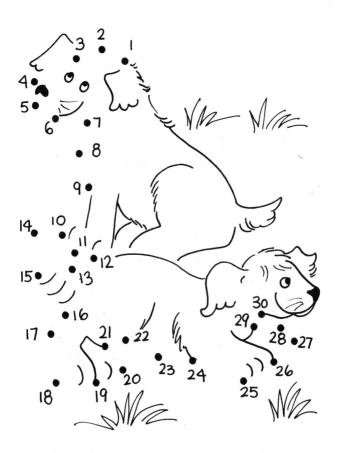

When these animals get bigger, they will help
the farmer herd sheep, too.

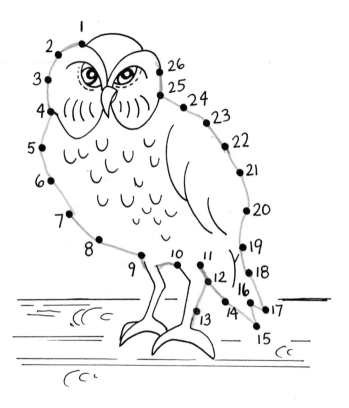

Not all farm animals live on the ground. From its perch in the barn, this bird calls out, "Hoot, Hoot!"

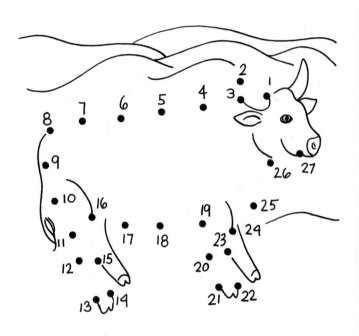

Large and heavy, this animal has a long, thin tail
and two big horns on its head.

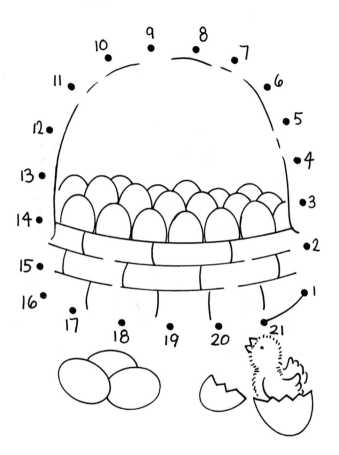

The farmer's wife will carry this into the kitchen
and put it in a safe place on the table.

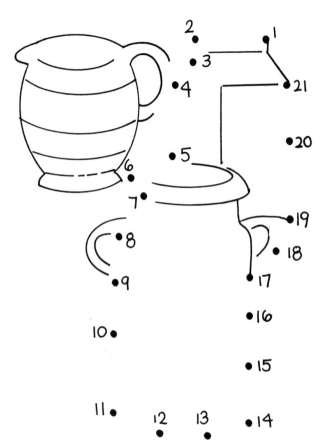

The cows make lots of this, fresh and sweet,
for the farm family to drink.

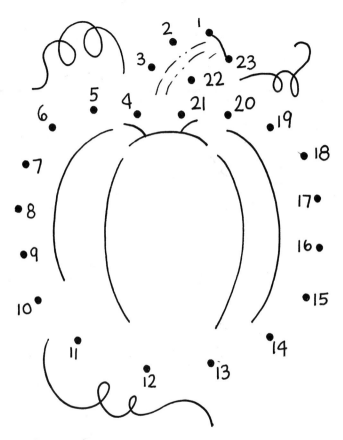

When you connect the dots, you will see a picture of a large orange vegetable that is popular at Halloween.

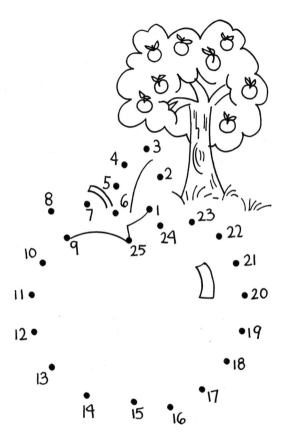

This shiny, juicy fruit grows on a tree.
The farmer's wife bakes pies using it.

This enormous pink animal likes to roll in the mud.
Like a pig, it has a curly tail.

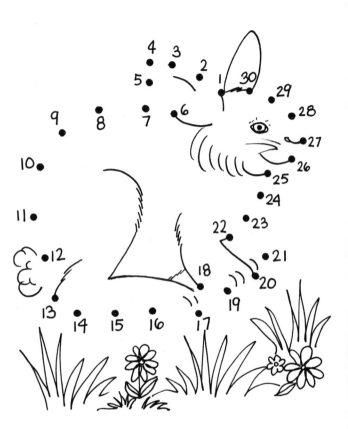

If you look carefully, you can spot this small animal.
It has a puffy tail like a cotton ball.

This tiny creature runs through the grass and hides in the barn. It keeps away from the cat and its kittens.

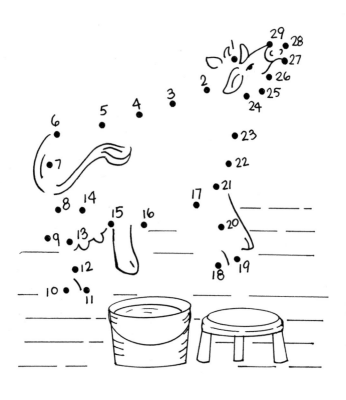

When it is milking time on the farm, this animal must be close at hand!

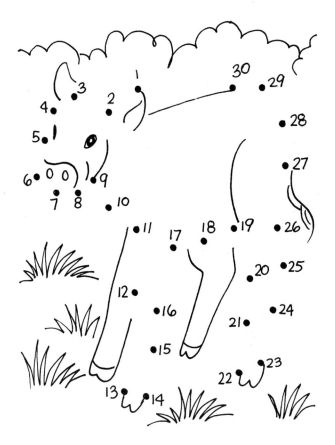

One day, this farm animal baby will find itself being led
into the milking shed. Follow the dots to see its picture.

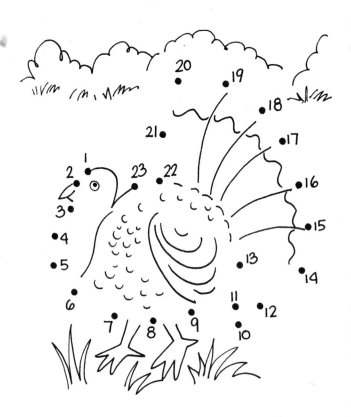

This bird is known for the sound it makes—
it sounds like "Gobble, Gobble."

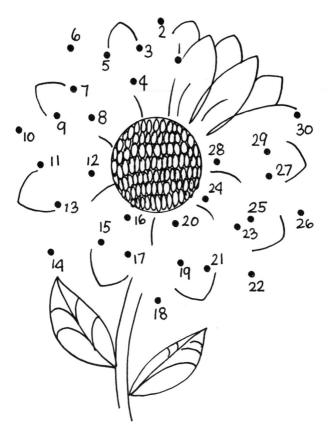

This flower grows very tall. Its large yellow petals surround its "head," which is full of seeds.

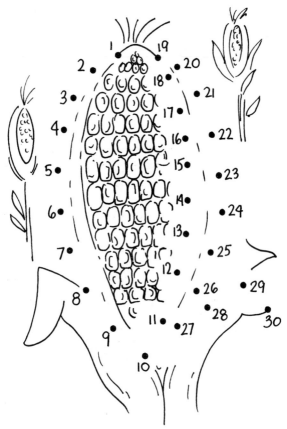

The farm has a field that has rows and rows of this
vegetable, which has "ears" inside of the outside leaves.

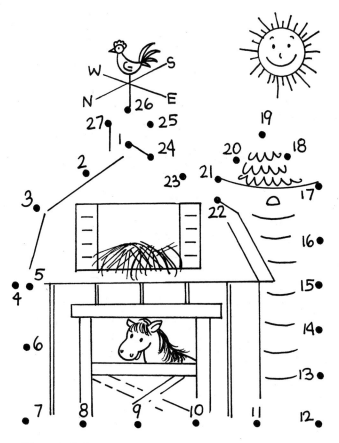

These buildings are used to house the animals and to
store grain. Connect the dots to see their pictures.

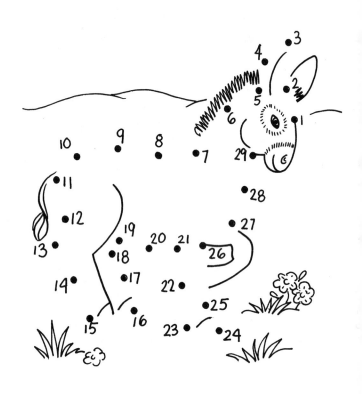

This horselike animal is one of the farm's work animals.
It may be used to pull a cart.

If you see this bird on a farm, you will be amazed
by the beauty of its colorful feathers.

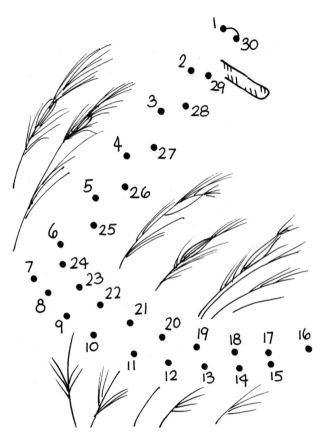

This farm tool has a very sharp edge. Be careful
when using it to cut the wheat!

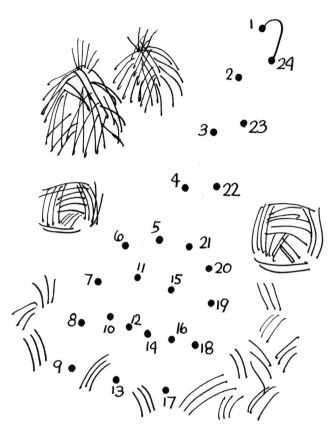

Its long, sharp "teeth" make this tool handy for
gathering hay for the horses.

This insect buzzes as it flies from flower to flower.
Follow the dots to see it.

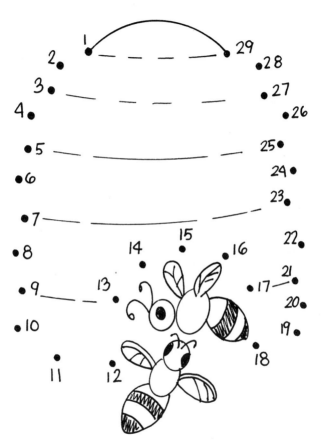

When this insect isn't busy working, it heads to this place,
where it lives with others of its kind.

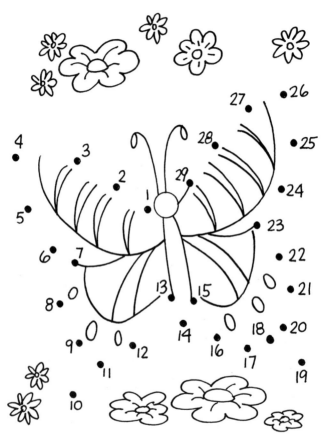

This creature is one of nature's most beautiful creations.
You can see it perching on a flower or a leaf.

If you hear the sounds "Quack, Quack," you will know that you are near one of these birds.

This baby bird makes a quacking sound, just like its parents. Connect the dots to see its picture.

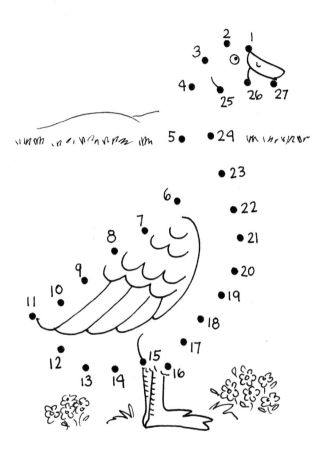

This large, white-feathered bird waddles around the barnyard, nibbling on grains of wheat and corn.

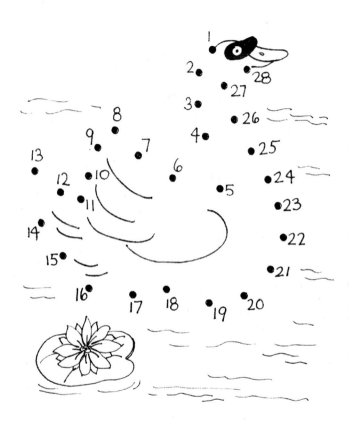

Swimming around in the pond, this white
bird looks very graceful.

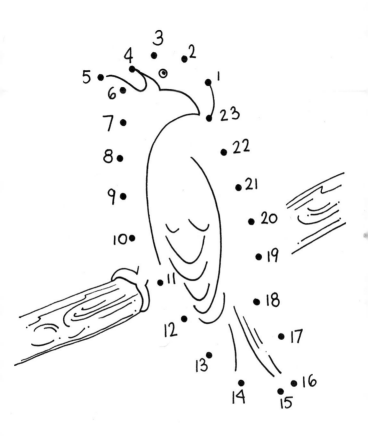

This bird is very helpful to the farmer, finding and eating many of the insects that might eat the farm's grain.

If there are puddles on the ground at the farm, you may
see this creature hopping from one puddle to the next.

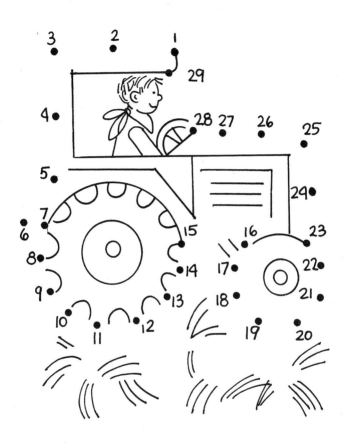

Connect the dots to see a picture of one of the most
important machines used by farmers.

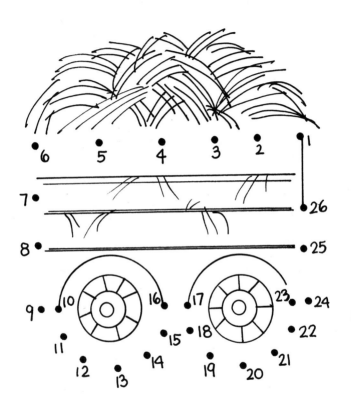

Here is some food for the horses. Find out what is used to carry it around the farm by following the dots.

Another type of work animal, this one can carry
a load or draw a wagon.

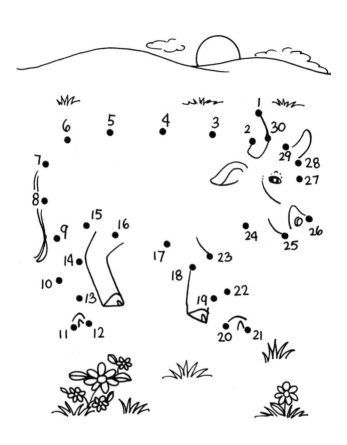

This large animal is so strong that it can pull a much larger load than some of the smaller farm animals.

It is the largest and heaviest bird. Although it has wings, it cannot fly.

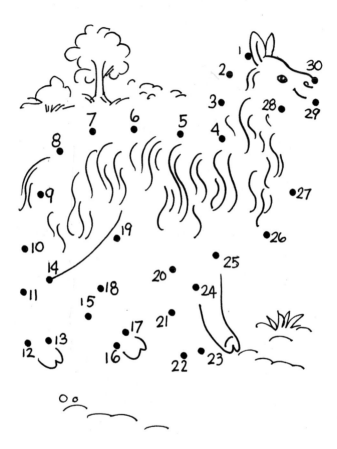

This animal, related to the camel, can be used for work as well as for its wool.

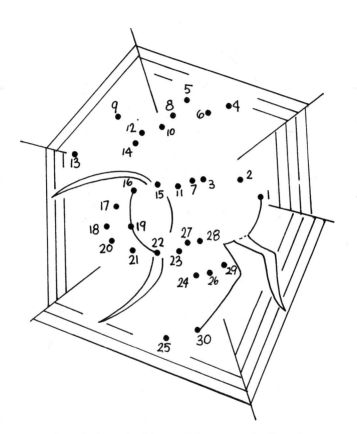

Snug in its web, this small insect can be found
in many places on the farm.

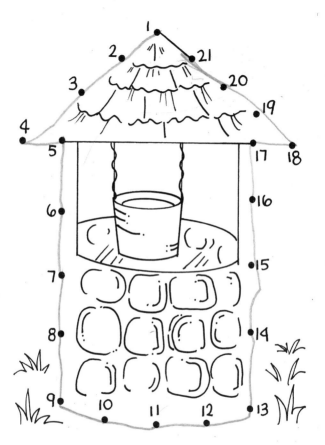

You will be able to draw water from the ground
when you lower the bucket into this.

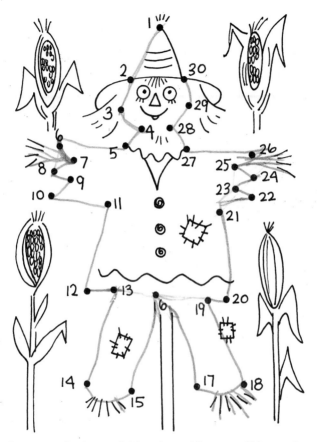

If you wander into a field and see this, you will know that the farmer is trying to keep the hungry birds from its corn!

Identifying
the Pictures

When you follow the dots, these are what you will find.